Renaissance Places

Sarah Howarth

The Millbrook Press
Brookfield, Connecticut

For Anne and Frank

Published in the United States in 1992 by
The Millbrook Press
2 Old New Milford Road
Brookfield, Connecticut 06804

First published in Great Britain in 1992 by
Simon & Schuster Young Books
Campus 400
Maylands Avenue
Hemel Hempstead
Hertfordshire HP2 7EZ

Designed by Neil Adams
Illustrations by Philip McNeill

Text copyright © 1992 by Sarah Howarth
Illustrations copyright © 1992 by Philip McNeill

Typeset by DP Press Ltd, Sevenoaks

Printed and bound by Proost International Book Co., Belgium

Library of Congress Cataloging-in-Publication Data

Howarth, Sarah.
  Renaissance places/Sarah Howarth.
    p.   cm.
  Includes bibliographical references and index.
  Summary: Profiles thirteen places during the time of the
Renaissance, from a chapel and sculptor's workshop to parliament
and deserted rural village.
  ISBN 1–56294–089–9
  1. Renaissance—Juvenile literature.   2. Cities and towns.
Renaissance—Juvenile literature.   [1. Renaissance.   2. Cities and
towns.]   I. Title.
CB361.H68 1992
940.2′1–dc20

92–7537
CIP
AC

Picture acknowledgments

Picture research by Caroline Mitchell

Front cover: National Gallery
Spine: Scala

Ancient Art & Architecture Collection: p.8, p.11, p.17, p.19, p.21, p.27, p.33, p.38, p.41
(bottom); Bridgeman Art Library: p.18, p.43, British Museum: p.9; Cambridge University,
Collection of Air Photographs: p.45; Mary Evans Picture Library: p.39; Werner Forman
Archive: p.31; Robert Harding Picture Library: p.15; Sarah Howarth: p.37; Mansell
Collection: p.12, p.13, p.16, p.20, p.25, p.26, p.28, p.44; National Gallery: p.24, p.29, p.35,
p.42; National Portrait Gallery: p.41 (top); Private Collections: p.23; Ann Ronan Picture
Library: p.32, p.34, p.36; Scala: p.7, p.10, p.14, p.30; ZEFA: p.22.

CONTENTS

Introduction 6

The City 7

The Sculptor's Workshop 10

The Chapel 13

The Printer's Workshop 16

The Theater 19

The Palace 22

The Library 25

The Parliament 28

The New World 31

The Observatory 34

The Monastery 37

The Home 40

The Deserted Village 43

Glossary 46

Further Reading 46

Index 47

INTRODUCTION

The Renaissance is a name given by historians to a time of great change in the fifteenth and sixteenth centuries. It was a time when there was a great deal of enthusiasm for the art and learning of ancient Greece and Rome. It was also a period of history that is especially famous for the works of art produced by painters, sculptors, architects, and craftsmen. Many of these people were influenced by the masterpieces of the ancient world.

This book describes places that were important to the people of the Renaissance. It will tell you about the places in which they lived, worked, studied, and worshipped God. It will also tell you about the people who designed and constructed their buildings, and about the events that took place inside them.

Many of the places described are in towns and cities. This is because the greatest changes of the Renaissance took place as towns grew and prospered. Wealthy merchants and traders made possible many of the developments of this period of history. They spent money on art, on new buildings, and to encourage the development of printing and research. They also paid for voyages of exploration and the search for new opportunities for trade. In time all these activities led to further and even more important changes.

THE CITY

We can imagine the busy atmosphere of a sixteenth-century city by reading these words from a letter written in 1504:

Wherever you turn your eyes, you see traders: confectioners, fishmongers, butchers, cooks, poulterers, fishermen, fowlers. On all sides houses block out the light.

This was written by the Englishman Sir Thomas More. He was describing the city of London, but the word picture he paints would have fitted many European cities at this time.

Here is a painting of the city of Venice. Venice had become rich because of the large amount of overseas trade that passed through its port. Shipbuilding was very important to the city. Thousands of workmen built ships there.

Growing numbers

In 1500 the largest cities were those of southern Europe, such as Venice and Constantinople. The population of each was about 100,000, an immense figure by the standards of the time. By 1600 several more cities had grown to this size, including London, Antwerp in what is present-day Belgium, Amsterdam in the Netherlands, Lisbon, Portugal, and Seville, Spain. The population of smaller cities, such as Florence in Italy, Vienna in Austria, and the German towns of Nuremberg and Ausburg, also increased. All over Europe, the urban (town) population was rising fast. The main reason for this was the large number of people

7

THE CITY

Here you can see a busy street scene. In many cities people were worried about keeping the streets clean. Look closely at this picture. Can you suggest why the streets might have been dirty?

moving from the countryside to the towns. They hoped to find work there—perhaps even to grow rich. But it was still unusual to live in a city. (Most people at this time lived in the countryside.) Only in Italy, Spain, Portugal, and the Netherlands did a significant proportion of the population live in towns.

Markets, warehouses, and sailboats

Many of the cities that grew and prospered during this period depended on international trade and finance. Amsterdam developed as an important European banking center, while Lisbon and Seville thrived on trade with the New World. A contemporary account of Venice in the sixteenth century—which describes the different markets there, the warehouses belonging to important companies of German merchants, and the sailboats arriving to sell fruit—shows us the life of another city that grew rich on trade.

London was one more city that flourished as companies of merchants were formed to engage in overseas trade. The "Merchant Adventurers" were among the most famous of these companies. Here one of the merchants tells of a journey he made in 1561:

Embarking in the ship Swallow *at Gravesend, we committed ourselves to God's protection. I arrived in Russia and sought permission to travel overland to Persia [Iran]. I was not permitted to do so because of war*

there. I spent most of the year in Russia, and sold most of the woolen cloths appointed for Persia.

This account reveals that overseas trade could indeed be an adventure. People went on journeys of exploration that could be dangerous in their search for new markets.

The Italian city-states

At this time, Italy was divided into a number of different states. In some of these states, one powerful city dominated the surrounding countryside: these were known as "city-states." The republic of Florence was one of the most famous city-states.

Trade had been important in Italian life for many centuries. The city-states of Italy grew rich, and their citizens looked for ways to express their pride in everything they had achieved. They did this by spending time and money on the creation of a beautiful environment. They paid for

magnificent new buildings, put up statues, ordered paintings and sculptures for their homes and public places, and passed laws to keep the streets clean. One example of these changes is given in a report on improvements in the city of Mantua, which was written in the sixteenth century:

Mantua used to be flooded with mud and stagnant water. Sometimes it was so bad it was fit only for frogs. Now it is transformed. Small tumble-down houses are pulled down, and bigger, better ones replace them.

During the Renaissance, projects were started to improve the appearance of many cities. Wealthy princes, merchants, and clergymen spent large amounts of money on such schemes. This picture shows Pope Sixtus V and some of the activities in which he was involved. He wanted to turn Rome into a magnificent city.

The Sculptor's Workshop

This is the voice of the famous fifteenth-century Italian sculptor Ghiberti:

In my shop are two pieces of bronze sculpture that I have made for a church in Siena. I calculate that they are worth about 400 florins. I also have a bronze casket in the shop that I made for Cosimo de'Medici.

Ghiberti was listing some of his possessions so that the city authorities could work out how much tax he should pay. His words give us a glimpse of a Renaissance sculptor and his workshop.

Sculptors performed many different sorts of work. Sometimes they were asked to make decorations for people's houses. The painting shown here was made to decorate a wooden chest.

Fountains and tombs

Renaissance sculptors produced some of their most magnificent work in Italy. For instance, in Perugia, the sculptor Giovanni Pisano worked on the fountain from which the city drew its water supply, making bronze and marble basins for it. *"Giovanni decided he had done this*

very well indeed and put his name to it," a sixteenth-century writer called Vasari tells us.

Some sculptors were commissioned (employed) to make tombs for important people. In Italy, Donatello and Michelangelo both took on work of this sort. Michelangelo (1475–1564) complained that the time he had to devote to the tomb of Pope Julius II ate up the best years of his life. In England the Florentine sculptor Torrigiano was asked to make a tomb when King Henry VII died in 1509. Nine years later it was finished, a marble tomb with bronze figures of Henry and his queen. It was the first monument in the Renaissance style to be made in England, and can still be seen in Westminster Abbey in London.

Everyday work

Not all the work commissioned from the Renaissance sculptors was on such a grand scale. Like other artists of the time, they also produced work for people's homes. Vasari describes how Donatello carried out commissions in this way:

He set his hand even to very small things. For example, he made coats of arms for the chimney pieces and fronts of town houses.

The evidence also shows us that even the greatest artists sometimes took on work decorating people's homes, painting beds, couches, chests, and other furniture.

Working as a sculptor

Sculptors learned their craft by being apprenticed to a working craftsman. When a boy became an apprentice, a contract was drawn up between the master craftsman and the boy's parents, setting out what the boy was to learn and various other arrangements. From records like these, we know that Michelangelo was apprenticed when he was a boy. As well as teaching him how to

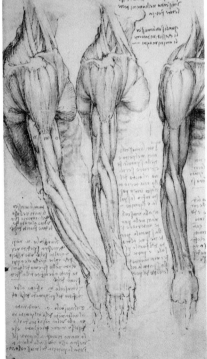

Like other artists, sculptors at this time wanted their work to look as realistic as possible. To achieve this, they studied the human body. This study of muscles in the arm and shoulder was made by the Italian artist Leonardo da Vinci.

THE SCULPTOR'S WORKSHOP

Here is a sculptor's workshop. Sculptors took orders for work from their patrons (the people who paid for the work). Sometimes all the details were written down in advance. This kind of arrangement was meant to prevent quarrels about how the work should be done. But there were often disagreements, all the same.

paint, Michelangelo's master sent him to study and copy the collection of ancient sculptures in the gardens belonging to the Medici family in Florence.

The apprentice had to learn many skills. One of these was how to make sculptures in bronze. One way to do this was to make a model in wax, with a core and outer casing made of clay. When the clay was hard, the mold was heated, so that the wax ran out. The sculptor then poured hot metal into the mold to replace the wax. Finally the outer clay mold was broken open. The bronze sculpture lay inside.

Casting great works in bronze was a very difficult business because of the possibility that something might go wrong. Here Vasari describes how Ghiberti cast the framework for the bronze doors he was making for the church of San Giovanni in Florence:

He made the mold very carefully and then dried it. He hired a room and built a huge furnace to cast the framework in bronze. Unfortunately it turned out badly. Ghiberti did not panic. He worked out what had gone wrong and made a new mold. This time it was perfect.

The work of famous sculptors like Michelangelo, Donatello, Ghiberti, and Torrigiano was commissioned by wealthy individuals all over Europe.

THE CHAPEL

Here a writer describes how the Italian artist, Michelangelo, completed his paintings on the ceiling of the Sistine Chapel in Rome, Italy. The work was commissioned by the pope:

The pope threatened that if Michelangelo did not finish it quickly, he would have him thrown off the scaffolding. Michelangelo hurried, and when the last pieces of scaffolding were taken down, the public was allowed to see it. This happened on All Saints' Day and the pope sang Mass in the chapel.

Art to honor and serve God

Many forms of art focused on the Church—painting, sculpture, architecture, music. In the Middle Ages these things were mainly concerned with religious purposes. They were supposed to teach congregations of people who had no education about their faith and they were

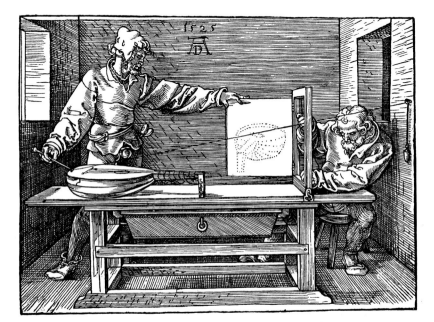

Here you can see an artist taking measurements. Like sculptors, Renaissance artists wanted their work to look realistic, and techniques like this helped. In the Middle Ages artists had different aims.

This fresco (a type of painting) was painted by the Italian artist Giotto. It tells a religious story and was painted for the Church. Many works of art were made for the Church at this time.

meant to glorify God. The tradition of art produced for the Church continued in the fifteenth and sixteenth centuries.

To find out more about this, let's look at the story of Michelangelo and the ceiling of the Sistine Chapel in greater detail. Pope Julius II asked Michelangelo to paint the ceiling of his private chapel in 1508, offering him 15,000 ducats for the work. The task was enormous. The fresco (painting) was completed in 1512 after four years' work. It illustrates scenes from the Old Testament of the Bible, from the Creation to Noah and the Flood. It is considered one of the greatest pictures in the world.

This story is an example of how the clergy supported the arts by commissioning great works for their churches. Popes like Alexander VI, Julius II, Leo X, and Paul III employed many famous artists of the time, such as Raphael, Botticelli, Bramante, and of course Michelangelo. One pope was said to have turned Rome upside down with his building projects, while plans to rebuild St. Peter's Church in Rome proved so costly that Pope Leo X paid for the work by selling special pardons for sin, called indulgences—something that many people disapproved of.

Music

Music was another form of art produced for the Church. It was composed especially for religious services like the Mass, or to accompany the singing of psalms. Many people thought that music was important in religious worship. The sixteenth-century English composer William Byrd put it like this: "*The better the voice, the better to honor and serve God, and the voice of man is chiefly to be employed to that end.*" Here again you can see the way in which people at the time looked on the different arts as ways of worshipping God.

Work deserving of praise

But this attitude was gradually changing. The Renaissance enthusiasm for human skills, talents, and achievements meant that the arts came to be regarded not only as a means of religious expression but also as activities in their own right. They were "*work deserving of praise,*" as one contemporary put it. Painting, sculpture, and architecture brought fame to their authors and prestige to their owners.

An historian who wrote at this time gives us a glimpse of this change. He tells us that Lorenzo, a member of the powerful Medici family in Italy, "*spent over 400,000 ducats building sumptuous churches and monasteries to immortalize his name.*" Church buildings were among some of the most famous new structures of the fifteenth and sixteenth centuries. The Pazzi Chapel in Florence and the Tempietto in Rome, for example, were designed by leading architects who followed new ideas that were taken from the architecture of ancient Greece and Rome. Buildings like these proclaimed the wealth and greatness of the city and its inhabitants.

Architects and artists showed a new interest in the classical architecture of ancient Greece and Rome. This is shown in the design of church buildings. Some of the most brilliant Renaissance artists worked on new church buildings like this.

THE PRINTER'S WORKSHOP

A sixteenth-century writer called Polydore Vergil had this to say about the printing press, an invention that interested his contemporaries a great deal:

As much may now be printed by one man in one day as could before scarcely be written by many in a whole year.

Before the printing press

In the Middle Ages all books were written by hand. This made them rare and also meant that it took a long time

Here you can see inside a sixteenth-century printer's workshop. By the window two men are getting the type ready for printing. At the front two men are working next to the printing press. The man on the right is putting ink on the type.

to produce each one. Many were extremely beautiful, their pages decorated with gold leaf and many colorful drawings. The monasteries of Europe specialized in painstaking work of this sort, because monks and other clergy were among the few people who could read and write at this time. Only by patient copying could they produce the Bibles and prayer books they needed.

Another writer describes a cleric: "*He was a very fine penman, and whenever he could snatch time, he busied himself writing a breviary [prayer book] with his own hand.*" Most medieval books were on religious or educational subjects.

The first printing presses

In China the art of printing was established in the ninth century. But in Europe it did not develop until the fifteenth century. The story there begins with a German goldsmith named Johann Gutenberg. In the 1430s he invented a way to print that used movable type. First the individual letters of the alphabet (the types) were made in metal. Then they were arranged into the words and sentences that were required for a page, and clamped together in a frame. Once the page was printed, the type could be taken out, rearranged, and used again.

To print a book, a printer set each page in type, rolled ink over it, laid it on the bed of the printing press, and put paper on top of this. Then he turned a large screw mechanism that brought a metal plate down on the paper, pressing it onto the type. The screw was undone after the page was printed and the press was ready for another sheet of paper. All this work was carried out in the printer's workshop.

Printing developed rapidly. Presses like Gutenberg's were set up in many parts of Germany, and German printers spread knowledge of the new invention throughout Europe. By the end of the fifteenth century, printing presses had been set up in many places, from London to Seville (Spain), Antwerp (Belgium), Paris, Stockholm (Sweden), and Cracow (Poland). In 1500 there were 150 presses in the Italian city of Venice alone.

What was printed

The printers first of all decided which works they thought would catch people's interest. Then they printed as many copies as they thought they could sell. If we look at the workshop of the first English printer, William Caxton, you will be able to see how they worked.

Caxton had learned about printing while he was in Germany and Belgium, and set up his own press in Westminster in London in 1476. He eventually printed

Printed books looked very different from manuscripts of the Middle Ages. The page here comes from a book printed in the sixteenth century.

17

This photograph shows a page from a book made in the Middle Ages. Historians call books like this "illuminated manuscripts." This means that they were handwritten and illustrated with brilliantly colored pictures.

about one hundred different books—some were translations he had made himself. The books ranged from popular books to entertain people, such as Chaucer's *Canterbury Tales* and Malory's tales of King Arthur, to works of scholarship. Caxton tells us how he decided to print Malory's work:

When I had accomplished and finished divers [several different] histories, as well as acts of great princes, many gentlemen came and demanded why I did not print the noble history of King Arthur.

A widening market

The work of printers like Caxton brought books to many people for the very first time. Books became less expensive, and as the quotation at the beginning of the chapter explains, many more could now be produced. In Venice, a scholar and printer called Aldus Manutius set up a press because he wanted to make copies of classical texts available to as many people as possible. He did this by printing and selling them as cheaply as he could.

THE THEATER

Here a sixteenth-century writer describes the opening of a new theater and the first play staged in it:

It was decided to build a theater according to the ancient custom of the Greeks and Romans. It can easily accommodate 3,000 spectators and cost 18,000 ducats. The most excellent tragedy ever written, Oedipus Rex, *by the Athenian poet Sophocles, was put on here.*

The new theaters

This account tells us about one of the very first Renaissance theaters. Palladio, the famous Italian architect, designed it in Vicenza, in Italy, and it opened on March 3, 1585. The people of the city were proud of their theater, which was considered one of Palladio's masterpieces.

Theaters were also built in other countries, such as England and Spain, at this time. The first English theater was built in 1576 in Shoreditch in East London and was called simply the Theatre. Others soon followed. One that later became especially well known was the Globe, built in 1599. The famous playwright William Shakespeare (1564–1616) was one of the actors there.

The picture drawn by a Dutchman

The theater at Vicenza was a particularly magnificent building. Others were more modest. We know what theaters like the Globe looked like because of a picture drawn by a Dutchman in 1596. It shows a circular building, with seats arranged in tiers (rows that slope upward) around the edge of the circle. These tiers of seats were called galleries, and the roof over them was made of thatch. The stage jutted out into the center of

This is the Globe Theatre in London. The Globe was one of the theaters that attracted large audiences in the sixteenth century. The playwright William Shakespeare performed there.

THE THEATER

This picture was drawn by a Dutch visitor to London in the 1590s. It shows us what the inside of many theaters looked like at this time. The actors are onstage performing a play, and a flag is being flown to show that a performance is in progress.

the circle, which was open to the sky. People could surround the stage on three sides to watch the performance. At the back of the stage was a "tiring room" for the actors to change in, and a tower. A flag flew from the top of the tower when a play was staged.

These wooden buildings were always at risk. Disaster struck at the Globe when a cannon that was fired as part of a performance set fire to the thatched roof and burned down the whole theater in 1613.

Plays on carts and in courtyards

Theatergoing soon became a very popular form of entertainment. Historians have calculated that at the end of the sixteenth century about 15,000 people each week packed the theaters of London. Even people who had little money could afford the cheapest seats, although the best seats were more expensive.

The Renaissance was the first time since the days of ancient Greece and Rome that buildings were designed especially for plays. Before the sixteenth century, plays had often been put on in the enclosed yards of inns, or simply on carts in the streets. This still happened in many places even after the new theaters were built. A letter written in Spain in 1579 describes how a mystery play (a play showing scenes from the Bible) was staged on a cart:

In one village, it was the custom on a special religious feast day for all sorts of entertainment to take place. Some of the people had made a cart on which they planned to hold a mystery play.

The plays

In the Middle Ages, few plays were staged. Like the mystery play put on in the Spanish village, most were religious and followed traditional patterns. This changed in the fifteenth and sixteenth centuries. People became interested in the culture of ancient Greece and Rome, and this led to the performance of plays by classical writers, particularly in Italy. The performance of *Oedipus Rex* at Vicenza is one example of this.

Classical writers had followed certain set rules. Influenced by these plays, some people now began to write their own works, too. Some of them deliberately experimented with the rules. For instance, by combining tragic and comic elements in one play, writers produced new forms of drama. William Shakespeare, the greatest English dramatist, and the famous Spanish playwright Lope de Vega both experimented with their writing in this way.

Elaborate shows called "masques" were put on at princes' courts all over Europe. They were very expensive to produce. The performers wore masks and magnificent costumes like those shown here.

THE PALACE

This description of a palace and its grounds was written in the sixteenth century:

The palace is a masterpiece of design. It has large grounds filled with garden and forest trees that are all beautifully arranged. It is laid out with charming groves, waters, fountains, fish ponds, fowling places, and espaliers.

Nobles and high-ranking people in many different European countries, from Hungary to England, created grand palaces like that at this time. The design of these buildings reflected the new enthusiasm for the classical architecture of ancient Rome. The new palaces were also more comfortable than the buildings in previous centuries.

Look at this photo of the palace of Chambord in France. Can you guess anything about the way of life led by its inhabitants?

From castles to palaces

In the Middle Ages, people with power and wealth lived in castles that were fortified against possible attacks. The most important consideration in building a castle was that it should be easy to defend. But now people began to build palaces that were splendid buildings meant for a leisurely life of pleasure and great ceremonies. This hints at a great change in the nobility's

way of life. Their time was no longer spent only or mainly in war. They became eager to display their wealth and position by collecting works of art and antiques, by giving extravagant feasts and keeping large numbers of servants. They also created beautiful palace gardens. Some palaces even had private collections of wild animals, but most owners just filled their gardens with many different kinds of trees and plants.

This description of a banquet in sixteenth-century Italy shows us the kind of life people led in the palaces of Europe:

The king gave a feast that cost over 150,000 florins. The guests ate from silver dishes. Fountains were set up that spouted fine wines. Silver cups were set next to the fountains for all to drink.

This standard of wealth and extravagance was not unusual. What impression do you think such a lavish entertainment makes on the guests?

Building palaces

The first palaces in the new style were built in Italy. Princes like the duke of Urbino—and sometimes even

artists, like Raphael—employed the most famous architects of the time to build palaces for them. These buildings won admiration, and soon the services of Italian architects were much in demand all over Europe. In many countries, palaces were built to follow classical designs, although some countries had their own design features. Let's look at a palace built in England and see what it can tell us about these developments.

The palace of Hampton Court

In 1514 work began at Hampton Court for Cardinal Wolsey, one of King Henry VIII's chief ministers. It was meant to be the largest house in the country, and the cardinal spent whatever money was necessary to get every detail just as he wanted it. For instance, although the palace could have taken its water supply from the Thames river, which was close at hand, Wolsey was afraid that the river was polluted and unhealthy.

Palaces were built to show the power and wealth of their owners. Many had collections of paintings, sculptures, and other works of art by the most famous artists of the time. The painting here is by an Italian artist for a palace in the city of Florence.

Instead, he commanded that the water be brought in lead pipes from streams more than three miles (five kilometers) away.

Craftsmen from several countries, including France, Italy, and the Low Countries (Belgium, Luxembourg, and the Netherlands), worked on the new building. They used some of the designs that were popular in their own lands, and so the architecture and decoration of the palace became a mixture of English and European styles.

The palace was so magnificent that it made Henry VIII jealous. So Wolsey, knowing that the king's temper could be dangerous, decided that he had better give Hampton Court to the king.

The rivalry between Henry VIII and Cardinal Wolsey makes the story of Hampton Court unique. But there are many other parts of the story that are typical of the time, such as the new approach to comfort, the desire to build a magnificent building, and the mixture of classical and traditional architecture.

THE LIBRARY

A bookseller from Florence in Italy describes one of his customers, who later became an English bishop:

His great collection of ancient books, and the others that he had copied for him, formed the beginnings of a noble library that he later founded in England.

A passion for books

This fifteenth-century Englishman had not only bought books from the bookseller in Florence. He had spent some time traveling through parts of Germany and Italy, studying and buying books wherever he went. His story is not unusual. A Hungarian bishop who had been sent to study in Italy bought Greek and Latin books in Rome, Florence, Venice, and Ferrara, and took them to start a library in Hungary. The bookseller in Florence also tells the story of an Englishman who bought so many books in Italy that he needed a ship to carry them home!

Pope Sixtus IV visiting a library in Rome. Many libraries were founded during the Renaissance.

Many libraries were begun at this time, most of them to house private collections of books. The first public library also appeared during this period. It was given by a member of the powerful Medici family to the monastery of San Marco in Florence in 1440. A contemporary noted these details: "*The library was 180 feet long and 36 feet wide. The shelves were made of cypress wood and filled with fine books.*"

Libraries were founded by clergymen, like the bishops from England and Hungary, by princes and powerful individuals like the Medici, and by private citizens. They were places that were intended for study. Today libraries lend out their books, but at this time books were so valuable that they were often chained down to stop people from stealing them.

Finding books in the wastepaper

You might have noticed that two details occur again and again in these stories. The first is that the books which collectors wanted so much were Greek and Latin texts. The second is that it was Italy, more than any other country, where people interested in Greek and Latin learning went. In Italy there were scholars, princes, and clergymen who were all eager to collect the works of classical writers and to share their enthusiasm with others.

The great interest in Greek and Latin books led to people discovering ancient works that had lain neglected for centuries. Some were found in monasteries, like a work by the Roman politician and writer Cicero, which was discovered by an Italian "*in a pile of wastepaper.*" This was not his only finding. Having traveled to Germany to attend a great Church council, he spent some time "*searching through the monasteries there for some of the books in Latin that had been forgotten.*" When he went home, he carried with him books of poetry and works on science, medicine, and many other subjects.

News about discoveries like these spread from Italy to

Books were valuable. They took a long time to produce and so were very expensive. If you look at this picture of a library you will notice that the books are chained down to stop them from being stolen.

other European countries and caused great excitement. Scholars wanted to have copies of these books. The way that the ancient Greeks and Romans studied the world was completely different from the approach taken by scholars in the Middle Ages. The Greeks and Romans had studied scientific subjects, making experiments and recording their observations. With the coming of Christianity, these subjects and this approach had seemed less important, and so Greek and Roman methods were no longer used. But in the fifteenth and sixteenth centuries scholars once more became interested in classical ideas and methods.

The renaissance (rebirth) of classical learning at this time aroused very strong feelings. Some people thought it was a sin to study ancient writers who were not Christians.

Teaching and learning

Many classical texts were translated so that they could be more widely understood. For instance, Cosimo de' Medici, a powerful Italian nobleman, encouraged a scholar named Marsilio Ficino to translate work by the Greek philosopher Plato into Latin. The study of such texts led to a new type of learning, known as "humanist studies." They were taught in Italy, and then taken up in other countries by scholars like the Englishman Thomas More and the Dutchman Erasmus.

Still, only a very few people were involved in the excitement and disputes surrounding the rediscovery of classical learning. Most people could neither read nor write at this time. However, education gradually became more common. One reason for this was the influence of Protestant leaders like Luther, Calvin, and Knox, and the work of the new Roman Catholic religious orders such as the Jesuits.

Fifteenth- and sixteenth-century scholars were passionately interested in ancient Greece and Rome. They copied many classical texts, some of which had not been studied for centuries. This edition of the Aeneid, a work by the Roman poet Virgil, was made in 1498.

The Parliament

Here a writer explains the work of a parliament held in the 1580s:

Parliament discussed how the person of the queen and the religion of the country could be protected against danger.

Today there are parliaments all over the world. They are assemblies in which people who have been elected to represent the opinions of others meet and decide how to run the country. These assemblies first developed during the late Middle Ages and Renaissance. As you will see, the first parliaments were very different from those we know today.

A question of power

King Henry VIII of England is shown here with his advisers. Parliament developed in England when rulers such as Henry asked their subjects for support. Important questions to do with war and religion led to discussions between the ruler and his or her people.

To understand the story better, we need to look at the way countries were governed at this time. Most European countries were monarchies; that is, they were ruled by a king or queen. Such rulers had very wide powers. In the sixteenth century some political thinkers put forward the idea that a king or queen was responsible only to God for his or her actions. They said that monarchs did not have to explain or excuse their decisions or actions to the people that they ruled over. Historians call this belief the "divine right of kings." You can see that ideas like this meant that there were no limits at all on royal power.

A place to talk

The word "parliament" comes from a word in the French language that means "to talk." Talking is what the first parliaments were all about. They were occasions when the monarch and his or her people met and talked about issues that concerned them. Such meetings allowed the monarch and his or her ministers to explain their policies to the country. They also allowed the voices of less powerful people to be heard for the very first time. This gave people the opportunity to protest with words rather than with violent actions.

Assemblies of this kind developed in a number of different kingdoms, such as France, Spain, Sweden, and England. But their powers varied greatly. Some kings and queens prevented parliaments from becoming too influential. It was in England that monarchs first found it necessary to cooperate with their parliaments, and that parliaments first began to have a say in the government of the country.

Making requests and granting taxes

In England, parliaments developed from the end of the thirteenth century onward. At that time the country was at war with France and the king needed to raise money to pay for the war. Before he could get the money, he had to explain to his subjects why the war was necessary. A few important knights were summoned from each county, and a few townsmen from each city. They came to the king and listened to what he had to say. They were asked to go back to their homes and raise taxes to pay for the war.

Parliaments were called whenever it pleased the king; there were no fixed times for them to meet. Sometimes the knights and townsmen brought questions and compaints on behalf of their neighbors. Gradually it became the custom for the monarch to listen to these problems, perhaps promising to make laws to resolve them, before the representatives of the towns and counties agreed to grant the taxes he or she had requested.

Noblemen like these were involved in governing their country. Some were sent to foreign countries as ambassadors. Their job was to look after the interests of their own land while they were abroad. Spying was considered one of their duties.

Sharing power

This fresco (painting) was painted for a public building in Siena, Italy. It is a painting with a political message and was meant to show people that it was important to have a good government. Many paintings and sculptures at this time had a political message.

In time parliament came to acquire power and importance of its own. For example, in England, King Henry VIII called many parliaments to ask for support for his decision to make the country break away from the Roman Catholic Church. The more often parliaments were called, the more they became an accepted part of English life. A king or queen who tried to rule without them would be unpopular indeed. Very, very gradually the ruler came to share power with the people, but the process was not completed for many centuries.

One nation

In the Middle Ages, people were more interested in the town or village where they lived than they were in their country. In the fifteenth and sixteenth centuries they began to have stronger feelings for their own particular country. They also began to be proud of it. We can see this new spirit of pride in the words of one sixteenth-century Englishman, who complained that the use of foreign expressions was *"debasing the King's English."* He was proud of his country and his language. Historians believe that the calling of parliaments was one reason for this growing feeling of nationalism.

THE NEW WORLD

In 1600 an Englishman, excited by the new voyages of exploration that Europeans were making around the world, decided to gather together all the facts he could about them. His name was Richard Hakluyt. This is what he had to say about America:

I shall write about part of the world sometimes called America, but also called the New World. It is called "New" for it was recently discovered by Christopher Columbus, a Genoese, in 1492. It is called "World," for it is huge, and it is even yet not thoroughly explored.

Europeans and the Americas

Columbus did not set out expecting to land in a continent that the Europeans had not come across before. His aim was quite different: he had hoped to find a new trade route to Asia. Columbus always believed that he had reached Asia, although he had in fact landed in the West Indies.

Some Europeans went to settle in the lands of the New World at this time, but full exploration of the mainland only came later. In the years after Columbus's death in 1506, the Spanish and Portuguese began to explore Central and South America. There was great rivalry between the two European countries and each one wanted to lay claim to these lands. In 1493, Pope Alexander VI tried to settle their quarrel by dividing the world in two, saying that any new territories to the west would now belong to the Spanish Empire, while those to the east would be Portugal's.

This Aztec mask comes from Mexico. It was made early in the sixteenth century and was used at Aztec religious festivals. The Europeans who traveled to America then found it very difficult to understand its people and their religion.

Sailors took their bearings to find their position by looking at the stars. This picture comes from a book that was printed in France in 1567. It shows a navigator studying the stars.

Rich mines of gold

In 1513 the Spanish explorer Balboa wrote a letter that gives us clues about one very important reason for the Europeans' exploration of the New World: the search for gold. He wrote: *"In Darien [in the Caribbean] there are many rich mines, with gold in abundance. Some say that all the rivers in the mountains contain gold."*

The discovery of gold changed European attitudes toward the New World. Men like Columbus had gone exploring because they were interested in trade. The aim of explorers like Balboa was to bring home as much gold and silver as they could find. These men were named "conquistadors," meaning "conquerors." The most powerful were two Spaniards—Francisco Pizarro, whose army conquered the Inca Empire of Peru in the 1530s, and Hernando Cortes, who led the conquest of Mexico, defeating the Aztecs.

The people of Mexico and Peru were forced to work as slaves to mine the treasure that the conquistadors wanted. Conditions were harsh and many people were killed. An English sailor shipwrecked there reported how *"The people have been cruelly treated. The Spaniards show no mercy."*

The gold and silver of the New World was shipped back to Spain. Each autumn the "treasure fleet" set sail with a cargo of precious metals for the Spanish monarchs, who were badly in need of this money. A contemporary described the fleet's arrival in 1596, saying: *"Three galleons [ships] have arrived in Seville, laden with two million gold pieces."* Historians believe that the huge quantity of gold and silver arriving in Europe at this time helped to cause inflation (a general rise in prices).

Mining for gold in South America. The first explorers wanted to trade, which would have benefited all involved. When the riches of the New World were discovered, the aims of the explorers changed. The people of South America were made to work as slaves to mine gold and silver. Many died because of the way they were treated.

Different ways of life

The first Europeans to arrive in America knew nothing of the people they found there. They could see that the way of life of the Inca and Aztec peoples was in many ways different from their own. As far as the Europeans were concerned, the most important difference was that these people did not follow the Christian religion. They found this horrifying. Members of the clergy followed the conquistadors across the sea. Religious orders, like the Dominicans, tried to convert the Inca and Aztec people to Christianity. But some also tried to improve conditions for the conquered peoples, and spoke out against the destruction of their age-old way of life.

This is the European side of the story. Do you think that the Inca and Aztec peoples would have taken a different view of the conquest of America?

THE OBSERVATORY

A book called *The Starry Messenger* that appeared in 1610 set out to:

Reveal remarkable sights in the moon and stars observed by Galileo Galilei, Gentleman of Florence, Professor of Mathematics in the University of Padua, with the aid of a spy-glass lately invented by him.

Galileo (1564–1642) was one of a number of astronomers whose observations caused fierce arguments at this time. Their work was to change the way in which people looked at the universe.

In the center of this picture you can see the castle of Uraniborg, built for the Danish astronomer Tycho Brahe. Built in the late sixteenth century, the castle contained laboratories and observatories. Brahe had many interests — from alchemy to astrology and astronomy.

Studying the stars

Astronomers were people who studied the stars. Knowing the position of the stars was important for sailors, who navigated (guided) their ships by observing where different stars were. In the days before clocks and calendars were invented, people also needed to know the stars' positions to tell the date and time. You can see this in a line from an old story of the Celts of Ireland: "*Cu Chulaind said to Leog, 'Go outside, and examine the stars and tell me if midnight has arrived.'*"

Most people also believed that the planets and their movements influenced everyday life. They thought that the pattern of the stars on the day someone was born affected what his or her character would be like. The stars were also supposed to affect health, so that doctors often wanted to know the position of the stars and moon before they treated their patients. Astronomers might be asked to supply this information.

Men like Galileo studied the stars for different reasons. They were breaking away from the old superstitions about the influence of the stars, and they had a more detached, scientific view of the universe.

They recorded what they saw, looked again—and again —and asked questions about the things they had noted. Did their observations suggest any patterns in the universe? Was there enough evidence for them to make a theory (rule) about what they saw? Galileo and others answered these questions with a definite ''yes.'' They were confident that they had discovered truths about the universe that no one had expressed before. But their beliefs were to lead them into difficulties.

Scholars at work. The Renaissance was a time when thinkers began to reject ideas that had been accepted for hundreds of years. Instead they carried out experiments, recorded their results, and finally put forward their own theories. Some people violently disagreed with the new ideas of astronomers like Copernicus and Galileo.

''I believe in the Holy Scripture''

During the Middle Ages it had been accepted that the earth was the center of the universe and that the sun, planets, and stars moved around it, each one following

a circular path. This view had been greatly influenced by the work of Ptolemy, a mathematician and astronomer who lived in Alexandria in Egypt in the second century A.D. Although some astronomers had noticed that this theory did not seem to fit exactly with what they observed, it allowed them to do their job and make calculations.

This picture of the universe was approved by the Church because it seemed to fit in with the words of the Bible. It was not only the Roman Catholic Church that took this view. Protestant leaders also believed that the universe was arranged in this way. "*I believe in the Holy Scripture where Joshua ordered the sun, not the earth, to stand still,*" said Martin Luther.

It was obvious that a theory that challenged the traditional belief would be met with great hostility.

New views of the universe

The first modern astronomer to put forward new theories about the universe was Nicolaus Copernicus, from Poland. His observations of the stars led him to suggest that the sun, not the earth, was at the center of the universe. His work was taken much further by Galileo, whose opinions scandalized the Catholic Church. Galileo was forbidden to express his ideas and he was put in prison. One important clergyman put the case against Galileo like this: "*To say that the earth revolves around the sun is a very dangerous thing, and injures our holy faith.*"

Here, *Tycho Brahe is shown with some of the instruments he used to study the stars.*

Breaking with the past

The work of famous astronomers, like Copernicus, Galileo, Tycho Brahe of Denmark, and Johannes Kepler of Germany, depended on careful observation. They did not just accept traditional ideas; in fact, they were prepared to reject theories that did not seem to fit the evidence. This was a revolutionary step. The methods of modern science developed from this way of thinking.

THE MONASTERY

Here a writer sums up the ideal of monastic life—the way it was hoped that nuns and monks would live:

They give alms [charity] to poor men and serve God. They teach the word of God, both by the example they set and by preaching.

Criticism and change

Very many religious houses were founded during the Middle Ages by men and women who wanted to worship God and lead holy lives according to strict rules. But as time went by, some of their rules and ideals were forgotten. Then people began to criticize those monks and nuns whose lives were not holy. For instance, some monks and nuns wore fine clothes, lived extravagantly, and did not spend any time in prayer.

The Italian writer Boccaccio, who lived in the fourteenth century, told many witty stories about the scandalous lives of nuns and monks like these. He was not the only person who had a poor opinion of monastic life. All over Europe people felt as he did. Changes finally came in the sixteenth century, as part of the great religious upheavals that transformed the entire Christian Church.

The ruins of Furness Abbey in the north of England. Many monasteries were dissolved (shut down) as part of the Protestant Reformation. Not everyone agreed that this should be done. In the north of England, for example, many people were unhappy about the decision to close houses like Furness.

Reformation and Counter-Reformation

People looked for change in other areas as well as in the monasteries. They were not satisfied with standards and teaching throughout the Church. Many people accepted the need for reform, but they disagreed about the way to achieve it. This problem divided the Church, and the Protestants broke away, refusing to accept the pope as their leader. Historians call this movement for reform the Reformation.

THE MONASTERY

Religious change caused anger that sometimes led to war. There was a war of words too. Books were written arguing for and against change. Illustrations backed up these arguments. This picture shows the devil talking to a monk. Its message was that the life led by monks was wrong.

The spread of Protestantism led the Catholic Church to undertake reforms of its own, too. A great Church council was held at Trent in the Holy Roman Empire to set out Church teachings and discuss reform. *"It shall reform what needs to be reformed,"* declared Pope Paul III. The Council lasted nearly twenty years. This Catholic movement of reform is known as the Counter-Reformation.

Both the Reformation and the Counter-Reformation brought great change to the monasteries of Europe.

Two solutions

Each Church had different solutions to the problem of reform. In Protestant countries, such as England, many parts of Germany, and Scandinavia, monasteries were closed. But this did not happen simply as a Church reform. It was a political decision as well.

In England, for example, King Henry VIII established the Church of England because he wanted to free himself from the pope's authority. Part of the reason for this was a growing feeling of national independence. Many people viewed the pope as a foreigner and resented the fact that he could influence events in their own country. An Act of Parliament of 1534 proclaimed that the king, not the pope, was the head of the Church in England. Then Henry introduced laws closing the monasteries because he feared opposition from the monks and nuns. He won support for this by breaking up the monasteries' rich estates and distributing them to the nobility and gentry.

In Catholic countries there were moves to reform monastic life, rather than abolish it. Pope Clement VIII hoped to set an example of the monastic way of life. One contemporary wrote:

The pope is determined to live a monk's life. He has had all carpets and ornaments removed from his rooms. In his bedchamber nothing remains but a bedstead, a table, and several skulls.

New religious houses were founded in which strict rules were followed. Many of these monasteries became known for their charitable and educational work. Two examples were St. Teresa of Ávila's Carmelite Order of Barefoot Nuns and St. Angela Merici's Order of Ursuline Nuns. The Ursulines played an important part in educating women.

Soldiers of Christ

One of the most famous of the new orders was the Jesuit Order, founded by St. Ignatius Loyola in Spain. Loyola had once been a soldier and he meant the members of his new order to be "soldiers of Christ." They took a vow of strict obedience to the pope. When Loyola died in 1556, there were Jesuit houses in many lands, from Italy, France, and Germany to India and Brazil. The Jesuits were especially interested in education and missionary work.

This picture shows St. Ignatius Loyola. Loyola founded a group of monks known as the Jesuit Order. The Jesuits worked to spread the Catholic faith.

THE HOME

In London in 1573 a man was hunting for a home for a friend. More than one house seemed suitable. Now it was time to write a letter describing those he had seen, and asking for his friend's decision. This is what he wrote:

I have found several having no furniture, and also several having such furniture as bedding, tables, stools, brass, pewter, and kitchen things. I need to know your mind.

Setting up house

Setting up house at this time was expensive. As the writer of this letter put it, *"Houses are very scarce and dear."* This meant that people could not get married exactly when they chose, no matter how rich they were. Young couples had to wait until they could afford to set up a home of their own, sometimes for years. It was not unusual for a young man to have to wait until his father died before he could marry. With the land inherited from his father, he would hope to set up house.

When a wedding took place, it was the custom for the girl's family to provide a dowry (gifts) for her to take to her new husband. A poet describes how one village bride brought with her *"many a pan of brass."* It was important for a family's pride to give a large enough dowry. For the wealthiest families, this might mean giving away a large amount of land or treasure. You can see that this custom was also something that could easily delay the wedding day.

Most young people were expected to marry a person chosen by their family. Few had a free choice. As one sixteenth-century Italian wrote on this subject:

It is the duty of the older members of the family— especially the mothers and aunts and grandmothers—

Here you can see a baby being looked after by its mother and a nurse. Many babies and young children died of disease at this time.

to choose suitable young women and introduce them to the young man. They should act just as they do when the family buys a piece of land, and look at all the advantages and disadvantages.

Marriage was arranged in a very businesslike manner. This was especially true among the very wealthiest people, who chose marriage partners to make themselves even more rich and powerful.

Childhood

During this period, families tended to be larger than they are in many parts of western Europe today. The Italian artist Leonardo da Vinci recorded that when his father died, he left ten sons and two daughters. It was not at all unusual for a woman to give birth to at least five or six children during her married life. Young children and babies were especially at risk from the many diseases that were common at this time, and many died in the first few years of life.

The family

In each family, the father was the most important person. His wife and children were expected to obey his wishes, and might be punished if they displeased him. A letter written by a noblewoman to her adult son in the

This is the tomb of an important family. It was made in the sixteenth century. Can you see the statues of the members of the family? How many children were there? Historians can use the evidence of monuments like this to find out about the past.

THE HOME

This picture was painted in 1434. It shows the betrothal (engagement to be married) of an Italian merchant and his future bride. Historians believe the picture was ordered so that the couple would have a record of what happened. The artist signed the picture. Can you see his name by the mirror?

fifteenth century gives us a glimpse of family life in those days:

You did not do well in leaving without my knowledge. Your father believes that I knew of your departure, and that has caused much trouble. I hope he will act as a good father to you if you are obedient to him. You must write as humbly as you can, asking him to be your good father.

This letter tells us a great deal about a father's authority over his wife and children. It also tells us something about the position given to women in society. Did they have the same powers as men?

THE DESERTED VILLAGE

One problem that worried people during the Renaissance was that land which had once been inhabited was now being abandoned. It was being turned into grazing land for sheep instead. A sixteenth-century lawyer wrote:

Sheep now eat up fields and houses. Their owners enclose all the land, throw down houses and leave nothing standing but the church.

Change in the countryside

The author of these words was Sir Thomas More (1478–1535), one of Henry VIII of England's most important ministers. But the events he wrote about did not happen only in England. In many European countries, such as Poland, France, and Germany, there were lands and villages that were deserted by their inhabitants.

The reasons for this varied from country to country. Historians believe that many places were deserted because the land was of poor quality for farming. It had been farmed previously, at a time when the population had increased so much that every inch of soil, however poor, was needed to grow food. But after the Black Death in the mid-fourteenth century, so many people died that this land was no longer needed, and it fell out of use.

The story in England was rather different. Here, too, there were deserted villages. But in many cases their inhabitants had been driven out; they did not leave because the land was poor. It was so valuable that their landlords wanted to farm it themselves.

This shows sheep being shorn for their wool. The wool trade was very profitable, but because raising sheep required fewer workers than growing crops, some country people found that they no longer had work.

43

Shepherds and their dogs

Raising sheep in England had become very profitable. Landowners could make more money by using land to graze sheep, and then selling the wool, than they earned by using it to grow crops. More and more landowners were beginning to keep sheep in the sixteenth century, and this led to great changes in country life.

Sheepraising required fewer laborers than growing crops did, and so some village people had no work. It was the first time that people in the countryside had been unemployed. Large areas of land were enclosed (fenced off) to keep sheep, and some landlords forced their tenants to leave their homes so that they could turn all their land into pasture.

Many people were troubled by the poverty and misery this created. One bishop put the problem in one area like this: *"In the past there have been many householders. There is now but one shepherd and his dog."*

Raising sheep was also very important in Spain, where great flocks were driven across the country to new pastures. Peasants here complained that the flocks trampled their crops.

For many people life changed very little during the Renaissance. They were not influenced by the new ideas or the new ways of life in the towns. Farming customs and life in the country changed only very slowly.

Tracing the deserted villages

The sites of deserted villages can sometimes be observed today. One of the clues to look for is a medieval church standing alone in the middle of fields. Most medieval churches were built to serve the needs of the

In some parts of Europe, land that had once been farmed was abandoned. The villages where the farmers had lived were left behind and became ruins. Sites where villages once stood can be seen most clearly from the air. This photograph shows the site of one deserted village. Only the church and manor house remain.

people who lived next to them. If a church is still there, but there is no sign of a village next to it, then the village may have been abandoned.

Photographs taken from airplanes and helicopters can also help in finding the sites of deserted villages. They show the marks left on the ground by buildings that stood for hundreds of years.

The pace of change

Many great changes took place during the Renaissance. However, the way of life of most country people was no different from the one their parents and grandparents had known. These people were not affected by the new journeys of exploration to distant lands; or by new ways of looking at the world that were followed by writers, humanists, astronomers, and political thinkers; or by the new, grander way of life in the cities.

But in the centuries to come, even life in the country did eventually change, and it was developments like these that laid the foundations of the modern world.

GLOSSARY

Alms Charity.

Apprentice A boy or girl who was sent to learn a particular trade or craft with a qualified trader or craftsman. There were many rules setting out what the apprentice would learn.

Astronomer Someone who studies the stars and planets.

Aztecs One of the peoples of Central America. Their empire in Mexico was conquered by the army of Hernando Cortes of Spain in 1522.

Black Death A disease that killed hundreds of thousands of people in the Middle Ages. At the time, no one knew what caused it. Scientists today believe that the Black Death was the bubonic plague.

Classical culture The art and learning of the ancient Greeks and Romans.

Dowry Gifts of land, money, or other valuable items that were presented to the groom and his family by the bride and her family when a wedding took place.

Enclosure Most land at this time was laid out in great unfenced fields. When land was enclosed, it was fenced off into separate plots. Many enclosures were made to keep sheep in.

Espalier A tree that is trained to grow in a special way along a wall.

Fortifications High walls and other defenses. They were built to protect places like towns or castles from attack.

Gold leaf A layer of gold as thin as tissue paper, often used for decoration on ornaments or furniture.

Holy Roman Empire The lands ruled by a prince known as the Holy Roman Emperor. Most of these lands were in modern-day Germany and Austria. Sometimes the emperor also had power in Italy and Switzerland. Because he ruled over such a large area, it was often difficult for the emperor to make all of the people in the empire obey him.

Humanist Writers and scholars who were particularly interested in the learning of ancient Greece and Rome. They based their own work on it.

Incas One of the peoples of South America. Their empire extended south from Ecuador to modern Peru and Chile. It was conquered by a Spanish army led by Francisco Pizarro in 1532.

Indulgences In the Middle Ages, many people believed that God would forgive their sins if they gave money to be used for a special religious purpose, like the building of churches. In return, the clergy promised them special forgiveness for sins. This forgiveness was called an "indulgence."

Inflation A general rise in prices.

Low Countries The area of northwest Europe where the Netherlands and Belgium are today.

Master craftsman A craftsman or woman who was especially skilled at their work. They had to pass many tests to prove their skill.

Merchant Adventurers A group of merchants and traders in London. They traveled to many parts of the world on business.

Missionary Someone who teaches people about their religion and tries to persuade them to follow it. Christian missionaries worked in the New World. They wanted the Inca and Aztec peoples to leave their own religion and become Christians.

Monastic orders Different groups of monks and nuns. Each order was slightly different and had its own set of rules. The order founded by St. Benedict was particularly famous.

Mystery play A play with a religious theme. In some mystery plays, scenes from the Bible were acted out.

Navigation Finding a way between different places. Sailors navigated their ships by using charts and looking at the position of the stars. These things helped them to work out where they were.

Pasture Grassland, used for animals to graze on.

Philosopher Someone whose work is to study and develop ideas about how people should live.

Scholar A person whose life is devoted to study and research.

Tiring room A room at the back of the stage in a theater, where the actors change in and out of their costumes.

Types The pieces used in printing. Each type is shaped like a letter of the alphabet.

FURTHER READING

Boyd, Anne. *Life in a Fifteenth Century Monastery*. Lerner, 1979.

Caselli, Giovanni. *The Renaissance and the New World*. Peter Bedrick Books, 1986.

Dwyer, Frank. *Henry VIII*. Chelsea House, 1988.

Hargrove, Jim. *Ferdinand Magellan: First Around the World*. Children's Press, 1990.

Odor, Ruth S. *Learning about Castles and Palaces*. Children's Press, 1982.

Raboff, Ernest. *Michelangelo Buonarroti*. HarperCollins Children's Books, 1988.

Richmond, Robin. *Introducing Michelangelo*. Little, Brown, 1992.

Sabin, Francene. *Renaissance*. Troll Associates, 1985.

Sendak, Cass R. *Explorers and Discovery*. Franklin Watts, 1983.

INDEX

Aldus Manutius, 18
alms, 37, 46
Americas, 31–3
Amsterdam, 7, 8
Antwerp, 7, 17
apprenticeship, 11–12, 46
architecture, 15, 22, 24
astronomy, 34–6, 46
Aztecs, 32, 33, 46

Black Death, 43, 46
Boccaccio, Giovanni, 37
books, 16–18, 25–7
Brahe, Tycho, 36

Calvin, John, 27
castles, 22
Catholic Church, 27, 30, 36, 37, 38
Caxton, William, 17–18
chapels, 13–15
childhood, 41
Church of England, 39
cities, 7–9
city-states, 9
classical culture, 15, 18, 21, 26–7, 46
Columbus, Christopher, 31
commissions, 11, 14–15
Conquistadors, 32, 33
Constantinople, 7
Copernicus, Nicolaus, 36
Cortes, Hernando, 32
Council of Trent, 38
Counter-Reformation, 38
Cracow, 17

divine right of kings, 28
Donatello, 11, 12
dowries, 40, 46

education, 27, 39
England, 29, 39, 43–4
Erasmus, 27

family life, 40–2
farming, 43–4
Florence, 7, 9, 12, 15, 26
fortifications, 22, 46

Galileo, 34, 35, 36
Ghiberti, Lorenzo, 10, 12
Globe theater, 19–20
gold, 32–3
gold leaf, 16, 46
government, 28, 30
Gutenberg, Johann, 17

Hakluyt, Richard, 31
Hampton Court, 24
Henry VIII of England, 24, 28, 30, 39
Holy Roman Empire, 38, 46
home life, 40–2
humanist studies, 27, 46

illuminated manuscripts, 16, 18
Incas, 32, 33, 46
indulgences, 15, 46
inflation, 33, 46
Italy, 8, 9, 26

Jesuits, 27, 39

Kepler, Johannes, 36
Knox, John, 27

land enclosure, 44, 46
Leonardo da Vinci, 11, 41
libraries, 25–7
Lisbon, 7, 8
London, 7, 8, 11, 17, 19
Low Countries, 24, 46
Luther, Martin, 27, 36

Mantua, 9
marriage, 40–1
masques, 21
master craftsmen, 11, 46
Medici family, 10, 12, 15, 26, 27
medicine, 34
Merchant Adventurers, 8, 46
merchants, 6, 8–9
Mexico, 32
Michelangelo, 11–12, 13, 14
missionary work, 33, 39, 46
monarchies, 28–9
monasteries, 16, 26, 37–9
monastic orders, 37, 39, 46
More, Sir Thomas, 7, 27, 43
music, 15
mystery plays, 21, 46

national pride, 30
navigation, 34, 46
Netherlands, 8
New World, 31–3
nobility, 22–3
nuns, 37, 39

observatories, 34–6

palaces, 22–4

Palladio, Andrea, 19
parental authority, 41–2
Paris, 17
Parliament, 28–30
pasture, 43, 46
Peru, 32
Perugia, 10
philosophers, 27, 46
Pisano, Giovanni, 10–11
Pizarro, Francisco, 32
plays, 21
Pope Alexander VI, 14, 31–2
Pope Clement VIII, 39
Pope Julius II, 11, 14
Pope Paul III, 14, 38
population growth, 7–8
Portugal, 8, 31–2
precious metals, 32–3
printing, 16–18
printing presses, 16, 17
Protestantism, 27, 36, 37–8
Ptolemy, 36

Reformation, 37
religious art, 13–15
Renaissance, defined, 6
Rome, 15

St. Ignatius Loyola, 39
St. Peter's Church (Rome), 15
scholars, 26–7, 46
science, 36
sculptors, 10–12
Seville, 7, 8, 17
Shakespeare, William, 19, 21
sheep raising, 43, 44
Sistine Chapel, 13, 14
Spain, 8, 31–2, 33, 44
Stockholm, 17

taxation, 29
theaters, 19–21
tiring rooms, 20, 46
Torrigiano, Pietro, 11, 12
trade, 8–9
types, printing, 17, 46

universe, theories of the, 35–6

Venice, 7, 8, 17, 18
Vicenza, 19, 21
villages, deserted, 43–5

Wolsey, Cardinal, 24
women in society, 39, 42
workshops, 10–12, 16–18

PRINTED IN BELGIUM BY

proost

INTERNATIONAL BOOK PRODUCTION